Reflections for the Effective Nonprofit Executive

A volume of the Effective Philanthropy and
Fund Raising series.

Reflections for the Effective Nonprofit Executive

Quotes, axioms and observations to help you manage our important institutions

Jim Norvell

Writers Club Press

San Jose New York Lincoln Shanghai

Reflections for the Effective Nonprofit Executive
Quotes, axioms and observations to help you manage our important
institutions

Writers Club Press
an imprint of iUniverse, Inc.

For information address:
iUniverse, Inc.
5220 S. 16th St., Suite 200
Lincoln, NE 68512
www.iuniverse.com

Artistic license was exercised with the quotes borrowed from an illustrious array
of thoughtful people. Insertion of their observations in juxtaposition to my
own was based on their unique similarity, often taken out of context. Those
who are still around to do so are free to do the same with mine.

ISBN: 0-595-20874-6

Printed in the United States of America

For Christie
At the center of all that is reflected in this book is my wife, Dr. Christine Norvell, who has been one of our nation's most important nonprofit executives for nearly 20 years—a public school principal. Her dedication to the teaching profession and unsurpassed skill at school management belies the indictment of our educational system as inept and ineffective.

Things do not happen. They are made to happen.

John Fitzgerald Kennedy

Something to believe in

Over a lifetime of nonprofit fund-raising management and consulting, I have been exposed to a wide spectrum of executive types. I have observed each to identify the attributes and skills that enable them to excel or cause them to fail. I have found no obvious locus. Race, gender, age, sexual preferences do not delineate. Personality types are undependable predictors. Neither education nor intelligence reliably classifies them.

Two distinguishing characteristics consistently present are a magnetic vision and an indomitable will. The best have a clear and determined ambition for the organization and make all around them feel crucial to its success. The effective executive's identity becomes synonymous with the organization. They provide that one thing that we all want—something to believe in.

The effective executives I have known have had healthy egos. I suppose it is even fair to say that their egos are substantial, but they never allow their own confident self-worth diminish recognition of others. The most effective of them use their power to ensure that everyone in the organization shares credit for its success. They are shields against disruptive forces and reinforcement for camaraderie at every level. They know that a proud and happy organization is an organization that is driven to achieve a shared goal.

The effective executives know the value of a dollar but are guided by the knowledge the achievement is never without cost. They eagerly take risks when the odds are right and the goal is worth it. They have an almost mystical intuition about the time that the organization needs and is ready for a shift in direction, even mission. The best never look back but always to the new opportunities of tomorrow. They welcome competition because it sharpens mission-driven activities, surfaces new potential donors, and allows them to make sharp and favorable distinctions.

The effective executives are fund raisers' most effective tools. Boards of directors provide stable anchors to constituencies, but effective executives have cast a mooring line to the future. They see needs far earlier than we do. They provide us an opportunity to be a part of the growth of humanity. Their success is a magnet for fellow achievers and a blessing for others. They are a solid investment that attracts blue-chip money. The radiance created around their organizations is a beacon for those looking to give more meaning to their lives.

Jim Norvell

Quotes, axioms and observations to help you manage our important institutions

This book was compiled as a resource for nonprofit executives. It contains some of the key guidelines I have found to be useful in managing nonprofit organizations. It also provides some handy quotations that may be used in various pieces of organizational literature to motivate volunteers and staff. Finally, I wrote it because I like quotes and have found that many of you share that enjoyment.

The inequities of life demand philanthropy.

We must build a new world, a far better world—one in which the eternal dignity of man is respected.

Harry S. Truman

Social consciousness is the first step in a philanthropic solution.

We must have the press of the crowd to draw virtue from us.

Angelo Patri

If the gift does not affect the donor's life, it is merely a handout—not philanthropy.

Do not be conformed to this world, but be transformed.

Romans 12:2 (NRSV)

Philanthropy is created by the same drives that fuel competition.

All of our dreams can come true—if we have the courage to pursue them.

Walt Disney

Most philanthropy is based on emotion.

Emotion has taught mankind to reason.

Marquis de Vauvenargues

Philanthropy is the socialism of democracy.

Whoever has two coats must share with anyone who has none; and whoever has food must do likewise.

Luke 3:11 (NRSV)

The more social freedom we experience, the greater our need for philanthropy.

I believe we are here on planet earth to live, grow up, and do what we can to make this world a better place for all people to enjoy freedom.

Rosa Parks

Philanthropy is second only to the vote in embodying democracy.

*Money spent on ourselves may be a
millstone around the neck; spent on others
it may give us wings like eagles.*

Roswell Dwight Hitchcock

Philanthropy cannot bridge all social inequities; but, with government as an ally and enabler, it can minimize them.

*Giving away a fortune is taking
Christianity too far.*

Charlotte Bingham

The quality of life in the United States would be unexceptional without philanthropy.

If there is one word that describes our form of society in America, it may be the word—voluntary.

Lyndon Baines Johnson

Philanthropy is a quid pro quo transaction.

As the purse is emptied, the heart is filled.

Victor Hugo

Altruism is more likely to appear as instinctual heroism rather than charity.

*There are two perfectly good men; one
dead and the other yet unborn.*

Chinese proverb

A philanthropic transaction is a
valuation and an exchange.

Decide what you want; decide what you are willing to exchange for it. Establish your priorities and go to work.

H. L. Hunt

Self interest regulates all transactions, philanthropy included.

A man does not have to be an angel to be a saint.

Albert Schweitzer

The philanthropic exchange is not always apparent.

A bone to the dog is not charity. Charity is the bone shared with the dog, when you are just as hungry as the dog.

Jack London

Negotiation is common in major philanthropic transactions.

Let every eye negotiate for itself
And trust no agent.

William Shakespeare

The apparent motivation for generosity may be misleading.

Take egotism out and you would castrate the benefactors.

Ralph Waldo Emerson

Altruism is highly overrated.

Every major horror in history was committed in the name of an altruistic motive.

Ayn Rand

The Philanthropic Sector is a response to life's inequities and the need to serve.

Life has no meaning except in terms of responsibility.

Reinhold Niebuhr

Social consciousness is at the root of philanthropy.

*We will have to repent in this generation
not merely for the vitriolic words and
actions of bad people, but for the appalling
silence of the good people.*

Martin Luther King, Jr.

Philanthropic acts stem from resonance between the needs of others and personal value systems.

Many organizations are very clear about the needs they would like to serve, but they don't understand these needs from the perspective of the customers.

Philip Kotler

Philanthropy is a gift on one side and a promise on the other.

*A mind conscious of integrity scorns to say
more than it means to perform.*

Robert Burns

Everyone has needs that philanthropy meets.

*Trouble is a part of your life, and if you
don't share it, you don't give the person who
loves you enough chance to love you enough.*

Dinah Shore

Nonprofit privilege and a huge revenue
stream make philanthropy an inviting target
for government control.

Those who worry about the motives of the charitable bolster their own political attitudes or comfort themselves with their own miserliness.

Benedict Nightingale

Philanthropy is too often marketed only through fund raising.

I get fifteen or twenty letters a day for everything from Yugoslavian dog illnesses to marathon diseases. It numbs you. So you write off a check for twenty dollars to a charity to absolve yourself of guilt.

Anjelica Huston

Philanthropy is both a behavior and an ideal.

Be not merely good; be good for something.
Henry David Thoreau

We have an inherent need to reinforce personal values.

The poor don't know that their function
in life is to exercise our generosity.

Jean Paul Sartre

Need is the perception of deficiency and the opportunity to approach fulfillment.

A poor person who is unhappy is in a better position than a rich person who is unhappy. Because the poor person has hope. He thinks money would help.

Jean Kerr

Everything is a value judgment.

Values are the lens through which self sees the world.

Tom Reynolds

Personal values are not static, but changes are few and far between.

All change is not growth; all movement is not forward.

Ellen Glasgow

People differentiate nonprofits by evaluating them against their personal value systems.

Caring is personal. It is rooted in an individual's own set of values, concerns and aspirations.

Peter M. Senge

Instinctual response and the conditioning of experience shape human behavior.

Men are wise in proportion, not to their experience, but to their capacity for experience.

George Bernard Shaw

Personal needs are an effort to shape reality.

Reality is something that you rise above.
Liza Minnelli

Life is defined by the drive to fulfill personal needs.

The significance of man is not what he attains but rather what he hopes to attain.

Kahlil Gibran

Values evolve to regulate needs.

It's not hard to make decisions when you know what your values are.

Roy Disney

Individual values regulate decision-making processes.

Why does a man act as he does? What would be required for a man to act differently? The key to motivation lies in the realm of values.

Nathaniel Brandon

Choices reflect and reinforce deeply-held values.

We don't see things as they are, we see them as we are.

Anaïs Nin

We are uniquely defined by the way we
express our values.

A man is literally what he thinks.

James Allen

The perceived consequences of behavior are balanced against personal goals.

You can do anything in the world if you are prepared to take the consequences.

W. Somerset Maugham

Understanding group values increases likelihood of developing linkages.

Public opinion is a thermometer a monarch should constantly consult.

Napoleon I

We reveal our values when we tell others
what is important to us.

Friends are my heart and my ears.
Michael Jordan

Nonprofits should periodically research constituent values to understand the "mind of the market."

Grace is given of God, but knowledge is bought in the market.

Arthur Hugh Clough

Jim Norvell

Gifts reflect the donor's needs.

*Nobody has ever measured, even poets,
how much the heart can hold.*

Zelda Fitzgerald

Donors satisfy value-driven needs when they provide philanthropic support.

I have found that the best way to give advice to your children is to find out what they want and then advise them to do it.

Harry S. Truman

Donors have rights that organizations should look upon as obligations.

There's no such thing as a free lunch.
Milton Friedman

Situational ethics aren't ethical.

I think its better to come in second than to be impeached.

George McGovern

Character is the expression ethical standards.

In matters of style, swim with the current;
in matters of principle, stand like a rock.

Thomas Jefferson

Commitment to ethical standards defines organizations and people.

If ever I said,
in grief or pride,
I tired of honest things,
I lied.

Edna St.Vincent Millay

Influential leaders shape the organizational culture.

The manager administers, the leader innovates. The manager maintains, the leader develops. The manager relies on systems, the leader relies on people.... The manager does things right, the leader does the right things.

Forbes Magazine

Nonprofits must abide by ethical standards in a much more public way than private sector organizations.

Many people like to believe charities as dishonest as they are supposedly mismanaged. They actually prefer them that way, because it means that they do not have to feel guilty about their own lack of generosity.

Benedict Nightingale

Fund raising's fiduciary implications demand specific ethical standards of the highest magnitude.

The knights had to vow poverty, chastity, and obedience. They only kept the last vow.

Gen. George S. Patton, Jr.

Ethics are a contract between the organization and its constituents.

I only know that what is moral is what you feel good after and what is immoral is what you feel bad after.

Ernest Hemingway

Ethical conduct is influenced, but not guaranteed by standards.

My best friend is the one who brings out the best in me.

Henry Ford

The highest ideals demand the highest
standards of conduct.

*The ultimate test for us of what truth
means is the conduct it dictates or inspires.*

William James

The practical expression of power is
leadership, but the possession of power
does not insure leadership.

Power? The only power I've got is nuclear—and I can't use that.

Lyndon Baines Johnson

The chief executive must be the initial
change agent.

Imagination is the highest kite you can fly.

Lauren Bacall

Learning to be a good manager is much more difficult than learning to be an effective fundraiser.

Some people are so busy learning the tricks of the trade that they never learn the trade.

Vernon Law

Style is an important element of leadership.

Every man of action has a strong dose of egoism, pride, hardness, and cunning. But all those things will be regarded as high qualities if he can make them the means to achieve great ends.

Charles DeGaulle

The skilled executive makes only those decisions that cannot be delegated.

No easy problems ever come to the President. If they are easy to solve, somebody else has solved them.

Dwight David Eisenhower

A leader is a symbol as well as a participant.

I was not the lion, but it fell to me to give the lion's roar.

Winston Churchill

Building shared vision is the leader's primary role.

*The only limit to our realization of
tomorrow will be our doubts of today.*

Franklin D. Roosevelt

Complex decisions are seldom made without a high reliance on intuition.

The heart always sees before the eye can see.

Thomas Carlyle

Intuition is one of a leader's most important assets.

Seeing's believing, but feeling's the truth.
Thomas Fuller

Leaders inspire by communicating an exciting organizational future.

Our chief want in life is somebody who will make us do what we can.

Ralph Waldo Emerson

The best executives have a vision and a charisma that motivate peak performance.

If you have anything really valuable to contribute to the world it will come through in the expression of your personality.

Bruce Barton

The quality of staff is an accurate reflection of leadership.

To be an effective leader you have to turn all your so-called followers into leaders.

David C. McClelland

A strong leader's influence is sometimes gained more readily by keeping them out of the limelight

I have had enough.

Golda Meir

The more powerful the leadership, the higher the motivation.

Winning isn't the only thing but wanting to win is.

Vince Lombardi

The board members' highest duty is to insure their organization operates above all applicable laws.

In the search for ways to maintain our values and pursue them in an orderly way, we must look beyond the resources of the law.

Dean Acheson

Someone has to show the way for others.

Do it big or stay in bed.

Opera promoter Larry Kelly

Leadership can make or break a
campaign and its participants.

A team should be an extension of the coach's personality. My teams were arrogant and obnoxious.

Al McGuire

Strong boards are fund-raising boards.

A few highly endowed men will rescue the world for centuries to come.

John Henry Newman

A strong board is an accident without a good nominating committee.

Quality represents the wise choice of many alternatives.

Will A. Foster

If the board chair will not lead, who will follow?

I have always had a dread of becoming a passenger in life.
Princess Margrethe of Denmark

Board members whose only financial
experience is balancing their own
checkbooks have a difficult time making
strategic decisions.

Experience is in the fingers and head. The heart is inexperienced.

Henry David Thoreau

Organizational structure must allow for control.

Discipline is the soul of an army. It makes small numbers formidable, procures success to the weak, and esteem to all.

George Washington

Delegation of authority is fundamental to organizational control.

Never tell people how to do things. Tell them what to do and they will surprise you with their integrity.

General George S. Patton, Jr.

As the number of direct subordinates
increases, a manager's control decreases.

What you cannot enforce. Do not command.

Sophocles

Discipline falters quickly when lines of authority are unclear or overlap.

Confusion is a word we have invented for an order which is not understood.

Henry Miller

Weak managers tend to use authority as a security blanket.

Authority is never without hate.
Euripides

Commitment to shared values shapes the organizational culture.

*If you don't have a shared value system,
you don't have an inner source of security.*

Stephen R. Covey

The ideal nonprofit is professionally managed and volunteer led.

The test of a first-rate intelligence is the ability to hold two opposed ideas in the mind at the same time, and still retain the ability to function.

F. Scott Fitzgerald

Fund raising is best managed by experienced professionals and done by respected volunteers.

When the professional's fund-raising knowledge and management skills are combined with the volunteer's influence, the result is success.

James Gregory Lord

A weak fund-raising board is a deficiency that no paid fundraiser can overcome.

Life is something like a trumpet. If you don't put anything in, you won't get anything out.

W. C. Handy

Volunteers run from conflict.

Tranquility will roof a house, but discord can wear away the foundation of a city.
Ernest Bramah

A weak board is more damaging than a
weak executive.

*In rivers and bad governments, the
lightest things swim at the top.*

Benjamin Franklin

Weak boards generally come from weak chairpersons.

When people are free to do as they please,
they usually imitate each other.

Eric Hoffer

Board members provide leadership best through planning, stewardship and evaluation.

As for him who voluntarily performs a good work, verily God is grateful and knowing.

The Koran, Ch. 2

No one solicits as effectively as a committed volunteer, only the chief staff officer is a close second.

Ya gotta do what ya gotta do.

Sylvester Stallone (as Rocky Balboa in "Rocky IV")

No paid employee carries the credibility of a committed volunteer.

You give little when you give of your
possessions. It is when you give of yourself
that you truly gain.
Kahlil Gibran

About the Author

James R. (Jim) Norvell

Jim is a second-generation fundraiser who began his career immediately after graduating from Southern Illinois University—Edwardsville. He served in annual fund positions at Monticello College, the Foundation for Independent Colleges of Pennsylvania and Washington University before joining G. A. Brakeley & Co., Inc., Los Angeles, as a capital fundraiser. He left Brakeley to form his own capital campaign consulting firm, Development Management Associates, Inc. (DMA) and to earn his MBA at UCLA. Over fifteen years, he and partner Bob Zuer expanded DMA to $2 million in annual billings, serving clients throughout the Western United States, Great Britain and Australia.

0-595-20874-6

www.ingramcontent.com/pod-product-compliance
Lightning Source LLC
Chambersburg PA
CBHW030939180526
45163CB00002B/629